RACE
AND
SPORTS

POLITICS
AND PROTEST
IN SPORTS

BY DUCHESS HARRIS, JD, PHD
WITH CYNTHIA KENNEDY HENZEL

D0709093

Essential Library

An Imprint of Abdo Publishing | abdobooks.com

ABDOBOOKS.COM

Published by Abdo Publishing, a division of ABDO, PO Box 398166, Minneapolis, Minnesota 55439. Copyright © 2019 by Abdo Consulting Group, Inc. International copyrights reserved in all countries. No part of this book may be reproduced in any form without written permission from the publisher. Essential Library™ is a trademark and logo of Abdo Publishing.

Printed in the United States of America, North Mankato, Minnesota
092018
012019

THIS BOOK CONTAINS RECYCLED MATERIALS

Cover Photo: Liu Zishan/Shutterstock Images
Interior Photos: Marcio Jose Sanchez/AP Images, 5; Alan Warren/Houston Chronicle/AP Images, 8; Charlie Riedel/AP Images, 10; Tony Avelar/AP Images, 13; CQ Roll Call/AP Images, 17; AP Images, 20, 22, 26, 28, 36, 40, 48, 52, 57, 59, 66; Julie Jacobson/AP Images, 31; Charles Krupa/AP Images, 33; Al Messerschmidt/AP Images, 43; Robert H. Houston/AP Images, 45; Rich Clarkson/Sports Illustrated/Getty Images, 64; Harry Harris/AP Images, 69; Michael S. Green/AP Images, 73; Bill Kostroun/AP Images, 79; Matt York/AP Images, 83; Duane Burleson/AP Images, 87; Timothy Nwachukwu/Star Tribune/AP Images, 89; Vincent Thian/AP Images, 90; Ron Sachs/picture-alliance/dpa/AP Images, 93; Michael Probst/AP Images, 95; Jacob Kupferman/Cal Sport Media/AP Images, 98

Editor: Patrick Donnelly
Series Designer: Craig Hinton

LIBRARY OF CONGRESS CONTROL NUMBER: 2018947973

PUBLISHER'S CATALOGING-IN-PUBLICATION DATA

Names: Harris, Duchess, author. | Kennedy Henzel, Cynthia, author.
Title: Politics and protest in sports / by Duchess Harris and Cynthia Kennedy Henzel.
Description: Minneapolis, Minnesota : Abdo Publishing, 2019 | Series: Race and sports | Includes online resources and index.
Identifiers: ISBN 9781532116711 (lib. bdg.) | ISBN 9781641856232 (pbk) | ISBN 9781532159558 (ebook)
Subjects: LCSH: Protest movements--Juvenile literature. | Public relations and politics--Juvenile literature. | Racism in sports--Juvenile literature. | Race relations --Juvenile literature.
Classification: DDC 796.089--dc23

CONTENTS

WHO IS MORE PATRIOTIC?

On August 14, 2016, Colin Kaepernick ran onto the field with the rest of the San Francisco 49ers football team for a preseason game. Kaepernick had been the starting quarterback for the team since 2012. He led the team to the Super Bowl in 2013. The next year, he signed a $126 million extension on his contract with the National Football League (NFL) team.

The quarterback was recovering from an injury and not expected to play on August 14. As the team stood for the playing of "The Star-Spangled Banner," no one noticed as he remained sitting on the bench. The same thing happened the next week. His actions again went unnoticed.

The 49ers were back in action on August 26. Kaepernick again sat during the national anthem. But this time a photo shared on social media brought his silent protest to the attention of the press. When asked why he was sitting instead of standing and facing the flag, Kaepernick explained he wouldn't "show pride in a flag for a country that oppresses black people and people of color. To me, this is bigger than football, and it would be selfish on my part to look the other way. There are bodies in the street and people getting paid leave and getting away with murder."[1]

BLACK LIVES MATTER

Like thousands of others in the United States that year, Kaepernick was protesting police brutality and the unequal treatment of people of color by police and the judicial system. Over the past few years, a series of killings of black citizens, mostly young men, had turned the attention of the nation to inequalities in the treatment of white and nonwhite citizens.

The Black Lives Matter movement began with the 2012 shooting of Trayvon Martin. The 17-year-old was walking from a store to his father's home in Sanford, Florida. It was dark and drizzling rain. George Zimmerman, a neighborhood watch captain, was suspicious of the black teen in his hoodie. He called 911 and, against the advice of

A demonstrator holds a photo of Trayvon Martin, the Florida teenager who was killed by a neighborhood watch captain in 2012.

the dispatcher, followed Martin. Zimmerman claimed there was a fight and said he shot Martin in self-defense. The unarmed teen was killed.

Authorities at first decided not to charge Zimmerman because he claimed he had acted in self-defense. But rallies around the country pressured authorities to reopen the case. Zimmerman was charged with second-degree murder. After a high-profile trial, he was found not guilty. The jury ruled that Zimmerman had "stood his ground" and believed the prosecution did not prove that Zimmerman had not "feared for his life."[2] One juror who spoke anonymously after the trial said that Zimmerman had a right to carry a gun and defend himself and that she didn't think he racially profiled Martin.

Many people were enraged when Zimmerman was acquitted. Shortly after Zimmerman's acquittal, black activist Patrisse Cullors used the hashtag #BlackLivesMatter in a Twitter post. It became a symbol of the protest. However, unarmed black men and women continued to be killed. Incidents of police brutality and use of deadly force—and the protests that sprang up in response when the courts refused to indict police officers for crimes—made the news regularly.

Kaepernick was a well-paid professional athlete. He was respected for his ability on the field and liked by fans and teammates. He believed he should use his public platform

Not all fans appreciated the protests by Kaepernick and other players.

to address wrongs in the country. He could not ignore the issue of racism.

PROTESTING THE PROTESTER

Fans and NFL officials were divided over whether it was appropriate for players to use their high-profile public positions as means of protest. Many people claimed to be insulted by Kaepernick's actions. They said that sitting on the bench rather than standing and facing the flag during the national anthem showed disrespect for the flag and the country it represented. They believed it was especially disrespectful to veterans—many of whom had given their lives defending the country—and their families.

Others said that sporting events were not the appropriate place for politics. Stephen Moore in the *Washington Times* declared that "sports is an escape, a respite from the politics and the problems of the world. I think I speak for millions of sports fans: I don't want to turn to the sports page and get lectured about race relations."[3]

Owners of NFL teams were especially worried about tarnishing the patriotic image of the NFL. The league depends on revenue from fans who buy tickets and other

DID PROTESTS HURT THE NFL?

Fewer people watched televised NFL games in the weeks after Kaepernick's protest. But it is unclear whether his protest caused any real decline. Although some viewers may have boycotted games due to player protests, others may have watched in support. Ratings for NFL games had dropped the previous year, and the viewing numbers for 2016 had already shown some decline in the weeks before the protest. Other possible contributors to the decline include the availability of alternative methods of watching games and a declining interest in football due to awareness of concussions and the long-term damage the game causes its players.[4]

NFL merchandise. More important, the league brings in billions via contracts with corporate sponsors and fees paid by media outlets to provide coverage of the games. The NFL, with revenues of over $13 billion in 2016, is a huge business.[5] Controversy could cost the league money.

SUPPORTERS

Chip Kelly, the 49ers head coach, as well as many other NFL players and officials, supported Kaepernick's right to protest. Team management released a statement saying that even if they did not agree with the way he protested, they supported his right to free expression as guaranteed by the First Amendment to the US Constitution. After presidential candidate Donald Trump tweeted "Maybe he should find a country that works better for him" and suggested that NFL owners should fire players who disrespect the flag, many teams stood in solidarity for the right to free expression.[6]

FIRST BLACK NFL COACH

In 1989, the Los Angeles Raiders made Art Shell the first black head coach in modern NFL history. The only other black head coach was Fritz Pollard, who was named a player-coach in 1923, when the NFL was just beginning. Black players have long constituted a majority in the NFL. Integration in coaching was slow but is improving. The number of black assistant coaches rose from 14 in 1980 to 199 out of 610 in 2012. As of 2017, eight of 32 NFL teams had black head coaches.

49ers head coach Chip Kelly, right, *stood by Kaepernick during the protest.*

OTHER FORMS OF PROTEST

Kaepernick was one of many athletes to use a high-profile position to support Black Lives Matter. In 2014, five Saint Louis Rams football players walked onto the field with their hands over their heads. The gesture meant "Hands up, don't shoot," to protest the shooting by police of teen Michael Brown in Ferguson, Missouri. Although the Ferguson police department criticized the display, the players were not punished by the NFL or their team. LeBron James, Kobe Bryant, and other National Basketball Association (NBA) players wore "I Can't Breathe" shirts to show support for the cause after Eric Garner died at the hands of police in New York City. A policeman had put Garner in a choke hold while he pleaded, "I can't breathe."[7]

Nate Boyer, a retired member of the US Army Special Forces and former NFL player, suggested to Kaepernick that kneeling would be more respectful than remaining seated. Since Kaepernick did not intend disrespect for the military, the country, or the flag, he knelt during the next 49ers game, on September 12, 2016. Teammate Eric Reid knelt beside him. Another veteran who supported Kaepernick, Joshua M. Patton, said that his military oath was not to the flag or the national anthem but to the US Constitution, which protects all citizens' right to criticize the government.

The attempt to show respect by kneeling rather than sitting during the anthem did little to satisfy those who railed against the protesting players. Kaepernick stayed strong, explaining, "This is not something that I am going to run by anybody. I am not looking for approval. I have to stand up for people that are oppressed. . . . If they take football away, my endorsements from me, I know that I stood up for what is right."[8]

The United States has a rich history of athletes speaking their mind in the pursuit of civil rights for all Americans. Kaepernick is just one of many examples of an athlete willing to put his or her future on the line to protest injustice.

DISCUSSION STARTERS

- Do you think professional sports leagues should decide whether players must stand for the national anthem?

- Would you boycott a sport, a team, or its advertisers if you disagreed with the political actions of its players?

- Do you think Kaepernick's protest made a difference?

- Is kneeling before the flag an insult to the country? An application of First Amendment rights to free speech? What do you think, and why?

CHAPTER TWO

THE BEGINNING OF INTEGRATION

The integration of sports, like the integration of schools, public transportation, and other parts of society, had a rough beginning in the United States. In the late 1800s and early 1900s, most sports teams were segregated. White athletes played on all-white teams. Black athletes played on all-black teams.

The sport of boxing was segregated too. Jack Johnson was the world's unofficial black heavyweight champion. James Jeffries, a white fighter, was the official heavyweight champion. Johnson wanted to fight Jeffries for the title, but Jeffries refused to fight a black man. Instead, Jeffries retired in 1905 and turned the title over to a new white champion.

Three years later, Johnson finally found a white champion who accepted his challenge. In 1908, Johnson beat Tommy Burns to become the official world heavyweight champion. Many people were enraged, demanding that a white champion come forward to take down Johnson. It didn't help that Johnson enjoyed flaunting the money he made from fights and endorsements. He also dated white women, going against the norms of the time.

White commentators called for a "Great White Hope" to beat Johnson. Jeffries agreed to come out of retirement to fight for the title on July 4, 1910. Jeffries declared he was

JIM THORPE

Jim Thorpe was a member of the Sac and Fox Nation from Oklahoma. His parents died when he was young, and he was raised as a ward of the state. In the 1912 Olympics in Stockholm, Sweden, he won both the pentathlon and decathlon in astounding victories. Bill Mallon, the cofounder of the International Society of Olympic Historians, claims that his performance made him the greatest athlete of all time.[2] He was celebrated as a hero on his return to the United States. Yet the International Olympic Committee (IOC) stripped Thorpe of his medals because he had been paid to play minor league baseball in 1909 and 1910. This made him ineligible for the Olympics because he was not an amateur athlete. In 1982, the IOC gave Thorpe's family replica medals but never made his records official. The decision is still controversial because white players who played minor league baseball were not sanctioned and the IOC broke its own rules by not taking the action within 30 days of Thorpe's win. After leaving sports, Thorpe worked in Hollywood as an actor. He was instrumental in getting movie producers to use Native Americans to play Native American roles.

"going into this fight for the sole purpose of proving that a white man is better than a Negro."[1] Johnson won, sparking deadly race riots across the United States.

Later that year, the federal government passed the Mann Act, forbidding the transport of white women across state lines for an "immoral purpose." Johnson was found guilty of taking a girlfriend across a state line. He fled into exile for seven years but eventually returned to face a year's jail sentence. It would be more than 20 years before another black boxer won the title. But before then, the country would finally come together to support a black athlete against a common enemy.

Jesse Owens salutes the American flag after being awarded the gold medal for the long jump in the 1936 Berlin Olympics.

THE GERMAN DEFEAT

Although professional sports were largely segregated, some universities had recruited a few black players by the late 1800s. George Poage from the University of Wisconsin was the first black athlete to win an Olympic medal. He won bronze medals in the 200-meter and 400-meter hurdles in 1904. John Taylor from the University of Pennsylvania won Olympic gold in the medley relay four years later. But it was in 1936 that Jesse Owens brought the attention of the world to a black athlete on the political stage.

Owens showed his gifts in track and field at an early age, setting records in both junior high and high school. He was recruited by several colleges and attended Ohio State University, where he set several new world records in 1935.

The next year, the Olympic Games were held in Berlin, Germany. Tension was high between the United States and Nazi-led Germany. German chancellor Adolf Hitler intended to use the Games to prove the superiority of what he termed the Aryan race, the prime example being the tall, blond, white northern Europeans. Owens dashed this hope by winning four gold medals. He won the 100-meter sprint, the long jump, and the 200-meter sprint, and he was part of the winning 4x100-meter relay team. He came home an American hero.

Despite Owens's hero status, he still faced racism back in the United States. As he explained it, "When I came back to my native country, after all the stories about Hitler, I couldn't ride in the front of the bus. I had to go to the back door. I couldn't live where I wanted. I wasn't invited to shake hands

JESSE OWENS: LEGENDARY ATHLETE

In 1935 at the Big Ten track-and-field championships in Ann Arbor, Michigan, Jesse Owens accomplished one of the most amazing feats in sports history. Although he had a sore back from falling down stairs, he tied the world record of 9.4 seconds for the 100-yard dash. He then set world records for the long jump, the 220-yard dash, and the 220-yard low hurdles. And he did it all in less than 45 minutes.

Heavyweight champion Joe Louis stands over Max Schmeling after knocking down the German challenger in the first round on June 22, 1938.

with Hitler, but I wasn't invited to the White House to shake hands with the president, either."[3]

A SECOND GERMAN DEFEAT

The Americans and Germans were soon to meet on another sports battlefield. African American boxer Joe Louis had won the heavyweight boxing title in 1937. Hitler wanted to use a fight between Louis and Germany's Max Schmeling, a previous titleholder, to show Aryan superiority. The stakes were high as the fight scheduled for 1938 took on nationalistic and racial overtones. Louis defeated Schmeling, making him a national hero.

Louis enlisted in the US Army in 1942. He toured the country giving speeches and boxing exhibitions. During World War II (1939–1945), although the military was still segregated, Louis helped increase morale and donated money to military relief.

Louis kept his title until his retirement in 1949. As of 2018, he still owned the record for holding the title the longest. One of the most admired athletes of all time, Louis was awarded the Congressional Gold Medal in 1982.

SPORTS AND PATRIOTISM

Owens and Louis provided examples of how sports is often a platform for Americans to demonstrate pride in their country. In many ways, sports has become synonymous with patriotism. But this was not always the case.

How did patriotism and sports become intertwined? In the fall of 1918, World War I (1914–1918) was still raging across Europe. Millions of people had died in the war between the Central Powers—led by Germany—and the Allies, which included the United States. More than 100,000 US soldiers had been killed since the country entered the war in 1917. And then the government announced it would begin drafting Major League Baseball (MLB) players to fight in Europe.

On September 5, 1918, players and fans gathered in Chicago for Game 1 of the World Series. It promised to be a good game between the Boston Red Sox and the Chicago Cubs, but both players and fans were somber. The war raged on. And the day before, someone had bombed the Federal Building and post office in Chicago. Four people had died, and dozens had been injured.[4] It seemed there was little to cheer about.

"THE STAR-SPANGLED BANNER"

During the seventh-inning stretch, a band in the stadium began playing "The Star-Spangled Banner." Most people knew the song, but at that time it was not a tradition to play it at sporting events. "The Star-Spangled Banner" did not become the national anthem until 1931.

As the familiar notes began, a Red Sox player who was on leave from the navy turned toward the American flag and saluted. Other players followed suit by placing their hands over their hearts. The standing crowd began to sing. As the song ended, a mighty cheer went up. It was the most spirited part of the day.

Boston won the World Series, and the war ended two months later. The Red Sox began to play "The Star-Spangled Banner" at every home game. Other ballparks also began playing the song on special occasions. It became even more popular once parks installed speaker systems.

JACKIE ROBINSON

Like the rest of the country, America's favorite sport—
baseball—was segregated in the first half of the 1900s.
Some integrated teams formed after the US Civil War
(1861–1865), but the National
Association of Baseball
Players banned integrated
teams in 1868. African
Americans still played
baseball, but they played on
all-black teams.

The general manager
of the Brooklyn Dodgers,
Branch Rickey, wanted
to change that. He knew
that to integrate MLB he
would need to find a player
with exceptional talent
in the sport. It would also
require a man with a special
personality. He would have to handle the racial taunts of
fans and other players. Rickey's choice was Jackie Robinson,
because in his view, Robinson was "a Negro with guts
enough not to fight back."[5]

Robinson took the field as the first baseman for the
Dodgers on April 15, 1947. It was difficult in the beginning,

BACK OF THE BUS!

Jackie Robinson served in the
army from 1942 to 1944. He was
arrested and court-martialed in
1944 in Texas for refusing to give
up his seat and move to the back
of the bus. Black newspapers,
friends, and activists came to
his defense. He then worked as
an army athletics coach until his
honorable discharge in late 1944.
In his 1972 autobiography, *I Never
Had It Made*, Robinson admitted
he never sang the national
anthem as he stood before
baseball games. This was his own
silent protest.

Jackie Robinson changed baseball forever when he debuted with the Brooklyn Dodgers in 1947.

but Robinson's talent and gracious demeanor won over fans and other players. He was named National League Rookie of the Year at the end of his first season. Two years later, he was named the league's Most Valuable Player. Robinson had opened the door for black players. April 15 is still celebrated by all teams in the majors as the day that the racial barrier in professional baseball was broken.

After his retirement in 1956, Robinson used his fame and respect to further the cause of civil rights in the United States. "A life is not important except in the impact it has on other lives," Robinson said.[6] He gave speeches and wrote editorials in newspapers. He wrote letters to President

John F. Kennedy, stressing the importance of the civil rights movement. These efforts, along with those of other leaders such as Martin Luther King Jr., the most prominent civil rights activist of the time, convinced Kennedy to introduce civil rights legislation in 1963. The legislation passed after Kennedy's assassination.

ARTHUR ASHE

It would be many more years before other sports were integrated. Arthur Ashe was key to integrating one of the last bastions of sports segregation, tennis. He began playing the game on the segregated playground near his home in Virginia when he was seven years old. Ashe was recruited by the University of California, Los Angeles (UCLA) in 1962. The next year, he joined the United States team to play in the Davis Cup, the premier team-tennis tournament in the world.

AIDS SPOKESMAN

Arthur Ashe, the first black man to become the top tennis player in the world, was forced to retire in 1980 after he had a heart attack. He contracted AIDS from a blood transfusion during surgery. A private and quiet man, Ashe was at first reluctant to reveal the disease. He eventually became a spokesman for AIDS prevention and research before his death in 1993.

While serving in the army in 1968, the 25-year-old Ashe won the US Open. It was the first time an African American man had won the Grand Slam event, one of four major

Arthur Ashe celebrates after becoming the first black player to win the prestigious Wimbledon title in 1975.

tennis tournaments. In 1970, he won the Australian Open. He won Wimbledon in 1975, the first black man of any nationality to win the event.

The only prominent black tennis player of his time, Ashe was often shunned by other players. In the early 1960s, he was barred from entering a movie theater with his team. He was at first rejected by the prestigious West Side Tennis Club at Forest Hills, New York, although later he was accepted.

Like Robinson, Ashe was concerned with civil rights. He explained, "I want to do something for my race, but I figure I can do it best by example, by showing Negro boys the way. That's what Jackie Robinson and Willie Mays have done in baseball, Wilt Chamberlain and Bill Russell in basketball, Jim Brown in football."[7] He opened medical clinics for underprivileged children and started inner-city tennis programs.

South Africa, which remained segregated, barred him from the country. White players there did not want to play a black man. He eventually traveled to South Africa to give speeches opposing the country's policy of apartheid.

Early black athletes won over Americans with their dignity and talent. They helped integrate sports. They brought attention to civil rights in a steady, unthreatening way. But as they found their voice, black athletes would be viewed differently by white sports fans.

DISCUSSION STARTERS

- Why do you think some universities were willing to recruit black players at a time when most of society was segregated?
- In your opinion, were black athletes such as Jesse Owens and Joe Louis exploited by the United States?
- Why do you think track and field was integrated earlier than tennis?

CHAPTER THREE

THE RISE OF PROTEST

M uch of the early acceptance of black athletes joining sports teams in the United States came about due to nationalism. The entire country took pride in Jesse Owens and Joe Louis representing the United States in defeating the Nazis.

By the end of World War II, the NFL mandated that the national anthem be played at every game. Other sports followed suit. Some people complained when fans laughed or talked while the song was played. But in 1954 when the owner of the Baltimore Orioles decided to stop playing the national anthem due to this lack of respect, baseball fans protested. Playing "The Star-Spangled Banner" had become a patriotic tradition.

The military found great benefit in tying patriotism and pride in the military to something as popular as sporting events. Military might was on display with fighter-jet flyovers and paratroopers dropping onto the field in pregame ceremonies. Providing military personnel and veterans to present the flag was a great advertisement for the armed forces. It helped recruit new military personnel. It also encouraged people to support the military with taxes as well as donations to support military families and

Military displays have become common sights at American sporting events.

veterans. This was especially important in the late 1960s because the war in Vietnam was facing increasing criticism.

The military soon found that tying politics to sport was a two-edged sword. Patriotism and sporting events became tied together during World War I and World War II. But in the 1960s, patriotism and sports added a new element— protest. As the Vietnam War (1954–1975) went on with no end in sight, some fans remained seated to protest the war while "The Star-Spangled Banner" played.

Because patriotism and sports were so intertwined, sporting events became a platform for athletes to protest their concerns from civil rights to anti-war sentiments. Those who agreed with the positions the athletes took endorsed their efforts. However, those who disagreed often decided, with some hypocrisy, that sports and politics didn't mix.

THE RISE OF MILITANCY

The Civil Rights Act of 1964 legislated against segregation in public places and discrimination in hiring. But African Americans who hoped for an end to discrimination with the Civil Rights Act were soon disappointed. Although the law had changed, the racist attitudes of many Americans had not. Black people were still treated as second-class citizens when it came to being integrated into private clubs and even sports clubs. They faced high unemployment and unfair housing practices and were often segregated into black neighborhoods with substandard services.

The Black Panther Party was founded in 1966 to protest police brutality in black neighborhoods. Party members dressed in black jackets and berets. They organized armed black citizens to patrol neighborhoods and monitor police activities. More importantly, they emphasized black pride and the power of black people to organize and control their own communities.

The Black Panthers became equated with violence and hate after several clashes with police and violent internal strife. Their influence waned, but their black berets and raised fists of resistance left a lasting impression on society that would reemerge in the field of sports.

MUHAMMAD ALI

The athlete most famous for bringing political protest to sports was not part of the violent uprising against racism. He was Muhammad Ali. Born Cassius Clay in Louisville, Kentucky, in 1942, he started boxing at age 12. His natural talent and hard work, as well as his outspoken ways, made him one of the most famous sports figures and American icons of the second half of the 1900s.

Clay won the light heavyweight Olympic gold medal at the 1960 Summer Olympics in Rome, Italy. His confidence and exuberance made him a well-known and popular figure during the games. Four years later, he became the world heavyweight champion. He was known for his light-footed style in the

BILL RUSSELL

Bill Russell was an outstanding basketball player during the 1950s and 1960s. He was also the first black head coach in professional sports, becoming a player-coach of the Boston Celtics in 1966. Russell was an outspoken proponent of civil rights. In 1961, he and his teammates boycotted an exhibition game in Kentucky when a restaurant refused to seat them. He went to Jackson, Mississippi, in 1963 after the assassination of civil rights activist Medgar Evers to lead the city's first integrated basketball camp. Even after he retired, Russell remained involved in civil rights, saying, "The only athletes we should bother with attaching any particular importance to are those like [Muhammad] Ali, whom we can admire for themselves and not for their incidental athletic abilities."[1] In 2010, Russell received the Presidential Medal of Freedom from President Barack Obama.

Muhammad Ali trains for his heavyweight title bout against Sonny Liston in Miami Beach, Florida, in 1964.

ring. He also was a proud spokesman for his own ability and worth as a black American.

Like Louis, Robinson, and Ashe, Ali lived in one world as a sports hero and another world as a black citizen. However, Ali was not comfortable accepting that he was a second-class citizen outside of the boxing ring. In 1964, he joined the Nation of Islam, an organization founded in 1930 that combined some teachings of Islam with black nationalism.

Ali took a lot of criticism for joining the Nation of Islam. Elijah Muhammad, the leader of the religion from 1934 to 1975, believed that African Americans should remain racially segregated from whites. But Ali felt the religion better represented his views than Christianity, a religion that he felt had been forced on the black slaves in America. He took the new name of Muhammad Ali. He insisted that fans and reporters alike call him by his chosen name, Muhammad Ali, rather than what he termed his "slave name, Cassius Clay."[2] He remained proud of his heritage and beliefs and insisted on what the law could not provide: dignity for the black man.

THE CHAMPION CHALLENGES THE DRAFT

The cause of civil rights was just one of the issues coming to a head in the mid-1960s. In 1964, most Americans supported the country's involvement in the Vietnam War. But in the coming years the casualties mounted, and there seemed to be no end to the conflict. The policy that governed the draft, the method the US government used to select people to serve in the military, favored the wealthy. Thus, the brunt of the war effort fell on the poor, which often meant young black men.

Ali received his draft notice in March 1966. He claimed the status of conscientious objector. Conscientious objectors can refuse to serve in combat roles in the military due to deeply held moral or religious beliefs. Ali was claiming that his religion did not allow him to go to war.

Ali's local draft board refused to grant him the status of conscientious objector and ordered him to report for military duty. On April 26, 1967, Ali went to the induction center. When his name was called, he refused to step forward. He was arrested. Ali explained that he had no quarrel with the enemy soldiers, saying, "They never called me n*****, they never lynched me, they didn't put no dogs on me, they didn't rob me of my nationality, rape and kill my mother and father. . . . Shoot them for what? How can I shoot them poor people? Just take me to jail."[3]

DRAFT DODGERS

Draft dodgers were men who refused to go to war. At first they were vilified during the Vietnam War. Later, as more people turned against the war, they became heroes. In 1972, the last year of the war, more than 200,000 men refused the draft.[4] Many left the country. In 1974, President Gerald Ford offered to let men return if they would participate in public service for six to 24 months. In 1977, President Jimmy Carter gave a full pardon to any draft dodger who requested one.

THE DRAFT

About two-thirds of the young men who fought in Vietnam volunteered. The other third were drafted.[5] All young men were required to sign up with the Selective Service when they turned 18 years old. If the government selected your name, you reported to a local draft board. The members of the local boards were made up of community members who would decide who would be sent to serve and who would not. There was a lot of pressure on these board members to favor certain young men.

For upper-middle-class or wealthy families, it was easy to enroll in college to avoid the draft. As a result, most of the American armed forces in Vietnam came from poor or working-class backgrounds. Very few came from upper-class families.[6]

This economic difference translated into a racial difference since black families were more likely to be poor. In addition, black troops were more likely to be in combat roles in the army and marines rather than in the navy or air force, which suffered significantly lower casualty rates. In the first years of US involvement in the war (1965–1966), black people made up about 11 percent of the US troops in Vietnam but over 20 percent of US casualties.[7]

Ali was put on trial and was found guilty. He was sentenced to five years in prison and fined $10,000. He lost his license to box and was stripped of his boxing world champion title. During the next years, he stayed out of jail while his case was appealed. But Ali, once one of the most popular men in America, became one of the most hated men seemingly overnight for refusing to serve in the military.

Television commentator David Susskind summed up the feelings of many in the country when writing about Ali: "I find nothing amusing or interesting or tolerable about

NFL star Jim Brown was one of Ali's longtime supporters in his fight against racial injustice.

this man. He's a disgrace to his country, his race, and what he laughingly describes as his profession. He is a convicted felon in the United States. He has been found guilty. He is out on bail. He will inevitably go to prison, as well he should. He is a simplistic fool and a pawn."[8]

WAR AND CIVIL RIGHTS

Ali still had supporters. Top black athletes such as Bill Russell, Jim Brown, and Lew Alcindor (now known as Kareem Abdul-Jabbar) spoke up for him. Because his passport had been taken away and he couldn't box, he made money giving speeches at universities about opposition to the war.

Slowly, the country began agreeing with Ali. People wanted the war to end.

On April 4, 1967, Martin Luther King Jr. came out against the war. He gave a speech calling for an end to the bombing in Vietnam. He said there was a common link between the war protests filling the colleges and the civil rights protests against discrimination. By 1967, 16.3 percent of all men drafted were black, although they were only 11 percent of the civilian population. They comprised 23 percent of all combat troops in Vietnam.[9]

Ali turned the attention of the country to a problem that had a unique impact on the black community. The issues affecting black Americans would soon be given a much bigger stage, and the 1968 Summer Olympics in Mexico City would change the conversation forever. But before that could happen, black athletes had to decide whether they even wanted to participate in the system anymore.

DISCUSSION STARTERS

- Would you fight for your country in a war you considered unjust? Why or why not?
- Why do you think Jackie Robinson was embraced by the public but the public turned against Muhammad Ali?
- Only men are required to sign up for Selective Service. Do you think all citizens should sign up? Do you think all citizens should serve their country in some way after high school?

WOMEN OF COLOR
BREAK
THROUGH

Black women began to integrate into sports in the 1950s. They were largely shut out of the protests of the 1960s because the black male athletes often couched their protests in terms of the dignity and pride of the black man. In later years, black women became some of the greatest supporters of civil rights.

Althea Gibson competed in tennis at the US National Championships (now the US Open) in 1950. She was the first black player to compete at Wimbledon the next year and won at Wimbledon in 1957. Gibson did not consider herself a crusader, saying, "I don't consciously beat the drums for any cause, not even the negro in the United States."[10]

Wilma Rudolph won three gold medals in track at the 1960 Olympics. She won the 100- and 200-meter dashes and the 400-meter relay, becoming an inspiration to young female athletes. Rudolph went on to become a teacher and coach and founded the Wilma Rudolph Foundation to promote amateur athletics. She once said, "Winning is great, sure, but if you are really going to do something in life, the secret is learning how to lose."[11]

Jackie Joyner-Kersee won six Olympic medals, including three golds. She set the world record in the heptathlon in 1988. She also was a star basketball player at UCLA. After retiring, she started

the Jackie Joyner-Kersee Foundation, which provides athletic resources to at-risk families in the Saint Louis, Missouri, area.

Serena and Venus Williams took the tennis world by storm in the late 1990s. En route to becoming two of the world's top players, the sisters fought for equal pay for female athletes. The Williams sisters faced their own form of racism. The white competitors they beat were often given better endorsements because they were considered more marketable.[12]

ATHLETES TAKE A STAND

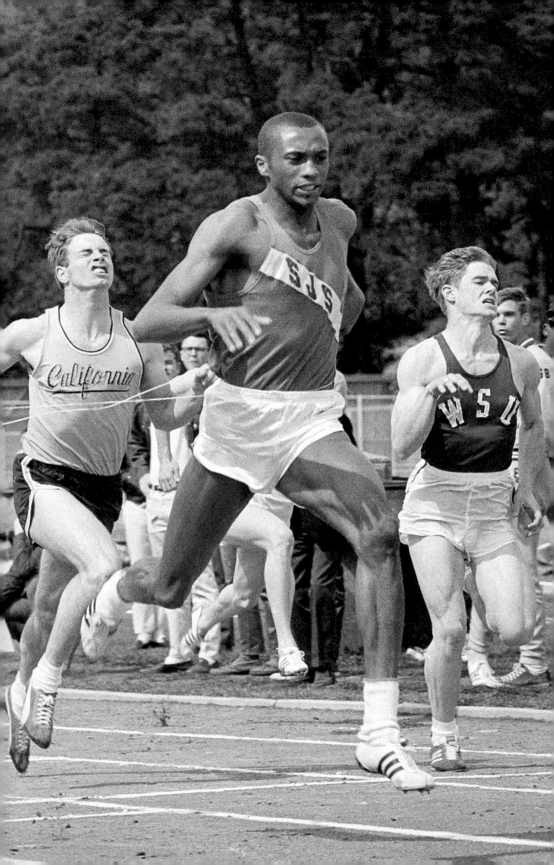

By 1967, black athletes were being widely recruited by colleges, especially in track and field. In the previous four Summer Olympics, black athletes had won more than one-third of the US medals in track and field. Still, these black athletes suffered from discrimination. They often found it difficult to find housing and were barred from many fraternities and other clubs. This was the case for black athletes at San Jose State College (SJSC) in California.

SJSC had one of the premier track teams in the country, known as Speed City. Among the elite sprinters on the team were Tommie Smith, Lee Evans, and John Carlos. Yet despite their sports fame, no one near the campus would rent a home or apartment to them because they were black. For these men, integration into sports was not enough. They wanted to use their position to gain equal rights in society for themselves and other black citizens.

Harry Edwards, a teacher at SJSC who was working on a master's degree in sociology, spearheaded the Olympic Project for Human Rights (OPHR) to protest the unequal treatment of black athletes. He met with black athletes to devise a plan to bring attention to their cause. One of the first athletes to take a stand with Edwards was UCLA basketball star Lew Alcindor. He outlined some of the racism he had encountered and then said, "This is how I take my stand—using what I have. And I take my stand here."[1]

DEMANDS

The OPHR came up with a list of demands. First, it wanted Muhammad Ali's world heavyweight title to be restored. Second, it demanded that Avery Brundage, head of the United States Olympic Committee (USOC) from 1929 to 1953 and president of the International Olympic Committee (IOC) from 1952 to 1972, resign his position. Brundage was considered a white supremacist by many. A millionaire himself, Brundage had no sympathy for those who wanted to change their status in life by earning money from their sports skills. He insisted that Olympic athletes remain amateurs, meaning they could not be paid for playing or earn money from endorsements.

The third demand of the OPHR was that the IOC

AMATEURS OR PROS?

Brundage competed at the 1912 Olympic Games in Stockholm. He placed fifth in the pentathlon and fourteenth in the decathlon. Both the pentathlon and decathlon were won by Jim Thorpe. Thorpe was required to return both gold medals later when Olympic officials learned that he had accepted a few dollars to play semiprofessional baseball prior to the Olympics, thus making him a professional athlete. Brundage, as head of the IOC, believed in strictly enforcing the amateur status of athletes who competed in the Olympics. Starting in 1988, the IOC allowed all athletes to compete.

A sign criticizing IOC president Avery Brundage hangs from a window of an Olympic Village building housing the US team in Mexico City in 1968.

disinvite the team from South Africa. Beginning in 1948, South Africa was ruled by a system called apartheid, an institution of severe racial segregation and discrimination. In 1964, Jan de Klerk, the country's interior minister, decided that South Africa would not integrate its Olympic team. The IOC withdrew South Africa's invitation to the Games.

Although apartheid was still the law in South Africa in 1968, the country had agreed to integrate its Olympic team. The IOC had invited them to participate in the 1968 Games. But other African countries planned to boycott the Games if South Africa participated because of the country's policy of apartheid.

The OPHR also encouraged a boycott of the New York Athletic Club, an all-white private club that hosted and promoted sporting events, and it asked for the hiring of more black coaches.

TO BOYCOTT OR NOT

The OPHR under Edwards knew that it would have to do something high profile

THE END OF APARTHEID

Apartheid in South Africa continued for almost 50 years. The country's ban on competing in the Olympic Games lasted 28 years.[2] In 1991, the IOC set conditions for the return of the country to Olympic competition, including the abolishment of apartheid. President F. W. de Klerk had already begun dismantlement of the policy, in response to growing protests and unrest in the country, and pledged to continue the effort. South Africa was allowed to compete in the 1992 Summer Games in Barcelona, Spain.

to get attention. The proposal he pushed was a boycott of the 1968 Summer Olympics by black athletes. A boycott by black athletes would have had a profound impact on the medal count of the United States. *Track and Field News* had predicted that 55 percent of medals in the coming 1968 Olympics in Mexico City would go to black athletes.[3] This was especially important at a time when the United States and the Soviet Union were fighting a cold war. A win for the United States was a win for democracy over communism.

Sports was viewed as a demonstration of democracy. Those who tried hardest and had the most talent would win.

The idea of a boycott appealed to some athletes, but others did not like the idea. The athletes who hoped to go to Mexico City had worked for years for the opportunity to compete on the world stage. For most of them, giving up this chance for an Olympic medal was giving up ever going to the Olympics. In four years, many would be past their athletic prime. Even for younger athletes, other opportunities after college or the responsibilities of marriage or children would keep them from competing.

Some people believed that the Olympics were the wrong place for political protests. The ideal of the Olympics was for the countries of the world to come together in peaceful competition and camaraderie. The Olympics had from the beginning given equal opportunity to athletes from every race. To protest racial injustice in the United States would tarnish this Olympic ideal.

As Brent Musburger from the *Chicago American* wrote, protesting at the Olympics

HARRY EDWARDS

Harry Edwards, the promoter of a black boycott of the 1968 Olympics, earned his PhD in sociology from Cornell University. He was then hired by the University of California, Berkeley. At Berkeley, he taught courses on race relations and the sociology of sport. Throughout his life he has worked with major league sports to improve racial relations. He is one of the most famous speakers and writers in the field of race and sport.

A fan protests treatment of black athletes at the 1968 US Olympic Trials in Los Angeles.

was "airing one's dirty clothing before the entire world."[5] The issue of racial discrimination was a problem in the United States. A black boycott of the Olympics would not only tarnish the country's reputation. It would divide the United States at a time when Olympic athletes needed the country's support.

THE DEBATE GOES ON

The OPHR under the leadership of Edwards continued to push for the boycott. There was no bigger stage to highlight the injustice done to both black athletes and citizens. For Tommie Smith, it was an excruciating decision. He was committed to using his position as a world-class athlete to help the black community. But would a black boycott of the Olympics really do that? Or was it an empty gesture that would accomplish nothing and cost him his chance for gold?

Even many of the pioneers of racial integration in sports were split on the matter of a boycott. Owens came out against it. Despite his fame for defeating the Nazis, he claimed that "there is no place in the athletic world for politics."[6] Louis said that the athletes should consider themselves Americans first and black Americans second.

Robinson, meanwhile, understood that playing the game did not mean equality. In his 1972 autobiography, I Never Had It Made, he wrote, "I cannot stand and sing the anthem. I cannot salute the flag; I know that I am a black man in a white world."[7]

THE NEW YORK BOYCOTT

As the winter of 1967 progressed, the OPHR could not get a firm commitment from its members on whether to boycott the Mexico City Olympics. The US Olympic track-and-field trials would be held in June. They would determine the athletes who would participate in the Olympic Games that October. The USOC, going against established practices, decided that those who won at the trials could be replaced at a later date. That way, if black athletes decided to boycott, the United States would still be able to field a team.

The OPHR got an opportunity to stage a preliminary boycott in January 1968. The New York Athletic Club sponsored a high-profile meet every year. Black athletes were encouraged to enter the meet, but they were not welcome to enter the door of the New York Athletic Club. The private club did not admit black members.

The OPHR helped promote a black boycott of the meet, but the boycott was not well organized. Word of the boycott spread more through word of mouth than through a highly organized endeavor. Some of the more militant black activists intimidated athletes to support the boycott. This led to questions about whether these methods of intimidation were better than the racism they hoped to quell. Some athletes did not hear of the boycott until the day of the event.

Despite the difficulties, the grassroots boycott was largely successful. All the high schools scheduled to participate pulled out. Only about nine black athletes competed. The OPHR was encouraged that an Olympic boycott might move forward.

DISCUSSION STARTERS

- Do you think the Olympics provide a proper venue for political protest?
- In your opinion, would a boycott of the Olympics have achieved the objectives of the Olympic Program for Human Rights?
- Would you give up your chance at an Olympic medal to protest injustice? Why or why not?

CHAPTER FIVE

THE WORLD STAGE

D ozens of protests by black athletes erupted on college campuses in the spring of 1968. Many black athletes still had to endure racial slurs from teammates, fans, and even their own coaches and trainers. They demanded equality on campus and in housing. Black athletes were often recruited with promises of financial help and tutoring. Sometimes the financial promises were broken. The athletes were encouraged to take a minimum number of hours of classes so they would have more time for practice. This meant that after four years, when their athletic eligibility, scholarship money, and tutoring help ran out, the athletes were not able to graduate.

Black athletes also demanded equal opportunities in college and professional sports. Although black athletes were recruited for their ability to win medals for their colleges and games for their teams, there was little opportunity for them to move into coaching or management. They felt that what they had to offer beyond athletic ability was ignored. In 1968, 23 black athletes at Iowa State announced they would withdraw from school unless the school agreed to hire black coaches. In team sports, black athletes were often denied the opportunity to play certain positions on the field. The most prestigious

From left, *Peter Norman of Australia, Tommie Smith, and John Carlos participate in the medal ceremony after the finals of the 200-meter dash in Mexico City.*

positions, such as quarterback in football, were exclusively reserved for white players.

As the protests continued, more and more athletes began to lean toward supporting an Olympic boycott.

Then, on April 4, one year after Martin Luther King Jr. had given his speech against the Vietnam War, the civil rights leader was assassinated. The grief and rage that followed encouraged many more to support the boycott. As track-and-field star Ralph Boston said, "For the first time since the talks about the boycott began, I feel that I have a valid reason to boycott. . . . I see that if I go to Mexico City and represent the United States I would be representing people like the one that killed Dr. King."[1]

Others, like Rafer Johnson, the 1960 decathlon gold medalist, wondered whether the sacrifice of giving up a chance to go to the Olympics was meaningful. He asked himself, "What good is it going to do? Is it going to help housing? Is it going to help education? Is it going to help job opportunities? I don't see how a boycott of the Olympics is relevant at all to these problems."[2]

THE FISTS SEEN AROUND THE WORLD

The boycott failed, with the exception of Alcindor, who made a personal choice to skip the Games. Still, the black athletes who attended the Mexico City Games felt a responsibility to use their platforms to achieve something for their people. Lee Evans had been an early supporter of the OPHR. As one of the leaders of the movement, he explained that they wanted to bring attention to the cause but did not want to protest the entire Olympics.

The athletes decided to wear a black article of clothing during each event they participated in.

Americans Tommie Smith and John Carlos took their marks on the track for the 200-meter dash on October 16, 1968. Smith won the gold with a time of 19.83 seconds, setting a new world record. Carlos took bronze. As the men waited for the medal ceremony to begin, Smith huddled with Carlos. Smith outlined his plan, and Carlos agreed to participate.

Smith's wife had brought a pair of black gloves to Mexico City. Smith now gave the left glove to Carlos. He kept the right glove for himself.

The two men walked to the medal platforms carrying their running shoes. They stepped up onto the platforms with only black

THE THIRD MAN ON THE PODIUM

The third man on the podium with Tommie Smith and John Carlos was Peter Norman of Australia. He had won the silver medal. Before the medal ceremony, Norman overheard the planned protest by Smith and Carlos and offered his support. He had seen intolerance in his own country. Australia had a long-standing policy of giving preference to white immigrants. The Americans gave Norman an OPHR button, and he put it on. Upon his return to Australia, Australian officials refused to put him on Olympic teams in the future even though he qualified. In 1972, they decided not to send a sprinter to the Games rather than send Norman. The country even refused to recognize him at the 2000 Games in Sydney, Australia. Norman died in 2006, six years before the Australian government issued an apology for its treatment of the best sprinter in the country's history.

socks on their feet. This, Smith later explained, represented the poverty and inequality of the black people in the United States. They wore black scarves around their necks as a symbol of black power and beads as a symbol of lynching.

As "The Star-Spangled Banner" began to play in the stadium, Smith and Carlos bowed their heads. Then they each raised a fist clad in a black glove. As the music ended, a few people in the crowd began to jeer. Some American athletes supported Smith and Carlos. Others were embarrassed or offended by their actions. The gesture was interpreted by many people as a symbol of black power. Smith later explained it was intended to show support for human rights and civil liberty.

AFTERMATH

Though few in the stands took notice, IOC officials were furious. The next day, the IOC asked that Smith and Carlos turn over their medals, but the men refused. The IOC then met with the USOC to demand the two men be disciplined. When the IOC threatened to send the entire US Olympic team home, the USOC suspended Smith and Carlos from the US team. They were ordered to leave Mexico immediately.

Lee Evans was tempted to leave also. But Smith convinced him to stay and win. The San Jose 400-meter runners did just that, with Evans, Larry James, and Ron Freeman sweeping all three medals in the 400-meter race.

FLAG PROTOCOL

The US Flag Code suggests that citizens who are not in the military stand and face the flag during the playing of the national anthem. The right hand should be placed over the heart. Men should remove their hats and hold the hat at their left shoulder so that their hand is over their heart. The code also mandates that the flag not be carried horizontally and not be used on advertisements. The flag also should not be worn as apparel and should not be used as part of a sporting uniform. These suggestions are often ignored. Images of the flag are commonly found on clothing and used by advertisers.

During the Vietnam War, the NFL created new rules to make sure its personnel did not follow along with protests. The new rules required all players to stand up with their helmets under their arms while the national anthem played. They could not talk, shuffle their feet, chew gum, or slam shoulder pads. In 2009, new NFL guidelines in the game operations manual stated that players were required to be on the field during the playing of the national anthem. However, before 2009, players in prime-time televised games often stayed inside their locker rooms until after the song [3]

The three men were warned by the USOC and the IOC of severe consequences if they followed the lead of Smith and Carlos. Still, they felt as if they had to do something to support the cause. They walked to the medal platform wearing black berets, a symbol of the Black Panthers. As they mounted the platform, they raised their fists and waved to the crowd. But once the national anthem began to play, they removed their berets and stood at attention until the song was done.

Other black athletes showed their support for the cause in their own ways. Bob Beamon, who took gold with a world

From front to back, *US athletes Lee Evans, Larry James, and Ron Freeman wear their black berets and their Olympic medals in Mexico City.*

record in the long jump, stood on the medal platform with his pant legs rolled up to show his black socks. Boston, who took bronze in the long jump, went barefoot during the medal ceremony. The IOC ignored the gestures.

BACKLASH

The anger against Smith and Carlos didn't lessen when they returned to the United States. They were ostracized by many in the sports community and criticized by much of the media for what many saw as a disgraceful display. Smith was discharged from the US Army.

Both men received death threats. Someone threw a rock through Smith's window. It almost hit the crib where his son was sleeping. They received threatening phone calls telling them to "go back to Africa."[4]

Using their international platform to bring attention to human rights cost them dearly. They lost any chance at endorsements or sponsorships. They never again competed at the international level. Many Americans considered Smith and Carlos the most hated athletes in the United States.

THE 1972 OLYMPICS

The IOC laid down strict guidelines for athletes during the 1972 Games in Munich, West Germany. It did not want a repeat of what had happened with the black American athletes in Mexico City. Smith and Carlos were barred from the Games, but Evans was part of the 4x400 relay team.

Vince Matthews had been part of the 4x400 relay with Evans in Mexico City. In Munich, he was racing in the 400-meter dash against fellow African Americans Wayne Collett and John Smith. Matthews won the gold and

A barefoot Wayne Collett, left, and Vince Matthews seem uninterested during the playing of the national anthem at the 1972 Munich Olympics.

Collett took silver, an injury to Smith preventing another American sweep.

The crowd and the officials watched as Matthews and Collett walked to the podium. Both had their jackets unzipped. Collett had bare feet. As the national anthem played, neither man faced the flag. They stood casually chatting, Collett with a hand on his hip and Matthews stroking his goatee. As the song ended, the crowd booed.

Matthews twirled his medal, and Collett gave a black power salute.

Brundage and the officials of the IOC were furious. They immediately barred both athletes from the Olympics for life, including the rest of the Munich Games. The USOC, after speaking to the men and determining they did not mean disrespect to the flag, tried to get the IOC to accept an apology. The IOC refused to discuss it. With John Smith injured and Matthews and Collett barred, the US had to drop out of the upcoming 4x400 relay.

Collett later explained his actions. "There are a lot of things wrong, and I think maybe the white establishment has too casual an attitude toward the blacks of America. They're not concerned unless we make a little noise and embarrass them."[5]

DISCUSSION STARTERS

- Why do you think Smith and Carlos were punished so harshly at the Olympic Games?

- Do you think it was selfish for Matthews and Collett to cost Team USA and teammate Lee Evans a chance at winning a medal?

- If African countries had boycotted the Olympic Games in Mexico City, do you think the American black athletes would have felt pressure to boycott, too? Why or why not?

CHAPTER SIX

THE BUSINESS OF SPORT

The years after 1968 brought changes not only to sports but to all of America. Protesters demanding civil rights, an end to racism, and an end to the Vietnam War filled the streets. Many of the protests centered on college campuses. The sacrifice made by Smith and Carlos galvanized college athletes, both black and white.

College athletes demanded an end to being treated as children. Instead of being given the same freedoms other young adults enjoyed, college athletes had no say in their own training, their education, or even how they dressed. Coaches and trainers could humiliate and degrade their athletes, and black athletes often took the brunt of these actions.

PROTEST SPREADS TO THE NFL

David Meggyesy, a linebacker for the Saint Louis Cardinals in 1968, made his own protest shortly after Smith and Carlos were expelled from Mexico City. The NFL commissioner had made a new rule about the actions of athletes during the playing of the national anthem. All players were to stand facing the flag with their helmets under their left arm and their right hand over their heart. Meggyesy held his helmet in front of him and bowed his head rather than face the flag as the anthem played. Meggyesy faced the same backlash as Smith and Carlos, but he stood his ground. "No one's going to give me an order about whether to face the flag or not," Meggyesy explained.[1]

Empowered by the example of people like Smith, they took action themselves.

On campuses across the United States, black athletes demanded fair treatment. In January 1969, five black football players at Princeton University charged their coaches with "racist tendencies" because black players were passed over for starting positions even though they played as well as white players.[2] The head coach resigned, and an interracial committee made up of faculty, students, and administrators investigated the issue and agreed on a new coach.

The demands of black players were not always met. When several black football players at the University of Wyoming asked to protest in a game against Brigham Young University, a white, segregated school, they were kicked off the team. Several black basketball players quit the team at Buffalo State due to racism.

AN UNEASY PEACE

After the 1968 Olympics, the OPHR slowly dissolved. Harry Edwards tried to keep the movement going. But with colleges willing to listen to complaints and the end of the Vietnam War, the social movements of the 1960s went quiet.

There were still isolated incidents. Louisiana State University (LSU) guard Chris Jackson was drafted by the Denver Nuggets of the National Basketball Association

(NBA) in 1990. He converted to Islam in 1991 and two years later changed his name to Mahmoud Abdul-Rauf. Abdul-Rauf refused to stand for the national anthem because it conflicted with his religion and personal beliefs about US military aggression.

Abdul-Rauf was suspended for one game before reaching a compromise with the NBA. He would stand for the national anthem, close his eyes, bow his head, and say a Muslim prayer. The move helped safeguard the team's playoff chances as well as Abdul-Rauf's $11.2 million contract. But it did not solve the issue of an athlete's right to express personal beliefs. As the *New York Times* stated, the problem was not Abdul-Rauf's view, but "the N.B.A.'s blindness to the fact that trying to force participation in a patriotic exercise undermines democratic values."[3]

As the United States prepared for war in 2003, a few athletes spoke up against fighting in Iraq. Basketball star Steve Nash wore a T-shirt during warm-ups that said, "No War. Shoot For Peace."[4] The next year, Toronto Blue Jays first baseman Carlos Delgado refused to stand for the playing of "God Bless America." Both men were savaged by fans and the media for those decisions.

MILLIONS AT STAKE

College sports in the decades of the late 1900s and early 2000s grew into a multimillion-dollar business, especially

Mahmoud Abdul-Rauf, center, prays silently during the national anthem before a game in 1996.

in the big moneymakers of football and basketball. As of 2013, the National Collegiate Athletic Association (NCAA) expected to cover up to 96 percent of its operating budget just from revenues from its annual March Madness national basketball tournament.[5] Meanwhile, universities are spending millions on stadiums and training facilities for their teams, even as tuition is rising at phenomenal rates and academic faculty often feel financial stress. Coaches routinely receive multimillion-dollar contracts. Former LSU basketball coach Dale Brown condemned the system as one that took advantage of the labor of "poor black kids."[6]

Student athletes, on the other hand, are provided a scholarship for tuition plus room and board. Training is a year-round commitment, so student athletes are not

THE SEVEN RICHEST COLLEGE SPORTS PROGRAMS

ATHLETIC DEPARTMENT REVENUE FROM 2016–17 FISCAL YEAR[9]

1. Texas, $214,830,647
2. Texas A&M, $211,960,034
3. Ohio State, $185,409,602
4. Michigan, $185,173,187
5. Alabama, $174,307,419
6. Georgia, $157,852,479
7. Oklahoma, $155,238,481

allowed to have jobs. They are not allowed to accept gifts. And their scholarships are actually just one-year agreements. This means athletes who are injured or who fall out of favor with the coaching staff can lose their financial support. As Desmond Howard, former University of Michigan football star, said, "[You] see everybody getting richer and richer. And you walk around and you can't put gas in your car? You can't even fly home to see your parents?"[7]

For black student athletes in the main revenue-producing sports at top schools, the outlook is particularly dismal. A 2016 study by the University of South Carolina's College Sport Research Institute showed that white football players graduated at a rate 5 percent lower than that of other full-time male students. But black players, who make up more than half of collegiate basketball and football players, graduate at a rate 25.2 percent lower than that of other black male full-time students.[8]

Taylor Branch, biographer of Martin Luther King Jr., argued, "The NCAA makes money, and enables universities and corporations to make money, from the unpaid labor of young athletes."[10] But for young men struggling to use sports to climb out of poverty, speaking out is as dangerous today as it was in the 1960s. It is, in fact, probably more dangerous because the stakes are much higher for those making money off the student athletes' performance.

PROFESSIONAL SPORTS

In 2011, both football and basketball players were locked out by team owners during contract negotiations. The conflicts between players and ownership often took on racial overtones. As of 2013, ownership of NBA teams was 98 percent white, while 76 percent of the players were black. In the NFL, there were no black owners, and 66 percent of the players were black.[11]

David Stern, the NBA's commissioner from 1984 to 2014, was at times criticized for actions that came across as racially insensitive. Hoping to make the NBA more appealing to white fans, Stern enacted a dress code for players being interviewed or sitting on the bench while not in uniform. Among the forbidden items were chains and baggy jeans, both popular with young black men.

Many fans had little sympathy for players with million-dollar contracts asking for more money. But players realized that their big checks didn't change the fact that they were one injury away from losing it all. The average career of a professional football player is 3.3 years.[12] Players who make it that far receive medical benefits for five years after retirement. For those who beat up their bodies week after week and often suffer multiple concussions, insurance can be hard to get. Medical problems are almost assured.

Eventually, players and owners came to an agreement, and the games went on. But owners soon had a new source of revenue.

PAY TO PLAY

Beginning in 2012, the US Department of Defense began paying teams to promote the US military during games. It essentially paid professional teams to market and advertise its "product." MLB, the NFL, the NBA, the National Hockey League (NHL), and Major League Soccer (MLS) accepted $10.4 million in government funds between 2012 and 2015.[13] For example, the Department of Defense paid the

Milwaukee Brewers $49,000 to grant the Wisconsin Army National Guard sponsorship of the singing of "God Bless America" at Sunday home games.[14] More than $6.1 million went to the NFL, where nearly 70 percent of the players are black. MLB, by contrast, received less than $1 million.[15] Less than 10 percent of its players are black.

The scheme was unmasked by US senators John McCain and Jeff Flake, both Republicans from Arizona. Although not illegal, giving taxpayers' money to wealthy sports franchises in order to turn patriotism into a commodity was unseemly. "Fans should have confidence that their hometown heroes are being honored because of their honorable military service, not as a marketing ploy," stated McCain.[16] The military discontinued the practice after it was revealed.

However, no matter how wealthy both amateur and professional sports teams became, they were soon forced to address issues of racism. There were still athletes willing to stand up.

DISCUSSION STARTERS

- Do you think "The Star-Spangled Banner" should be played to begin sporting events? Why or why not?
- Do you think the race of pro sports team owners should matter?
- Should college athletes be paid for playing sports? Should they be able to accept endorsement money or gifts? Explain your answer.

CHAPTER SEVEN

RACISM
CONTINUES

Black athletes are not the only victims of racial profiling. Basketball player Jeremy Lin found it difficult to get a chance to play because of his Asian American heritage. Lin, whose parents are Chinese Taiwanese, was an excellent player in high school. He went to Harvard, played well, and graduated with a degree in economics, but he was not drafted by an NBA team.

Lin felt that he was not given a chance because of his race. He did not fit the "look" of a top-tier player. Plus, he had gone to Harvard. People didn't believe a smart Asian man could also excel at sports.

Lin spent a year in the NBA's Development League, at the low end of the professional basketball ladder, before securing a roster spot with the New York Knicks in January 2012. Then, seemingly overnight, Lin became one of the most famous players in the world as he helped the Knicks salvage their season. He set the record for the most points in NBA history in his first five starts. Although a popular player, Lin still had to face racial slurs from opposing teams and even sportscasters.

LATINO PLAYERS

While football and basketball rosters are dominated by black players, baseball has seen a continued uptick in the number of Latino players at all levels of the professional game. Owners, managers, and players remain predominantly white. But in 2013, 28 percent of MLB players were Latino.[1] The number of Latino baseball players is growing as more teams establish academies in Latin America to recruit and train players.

Like others, Latinos face stereotyping. In 2011, San Francisco Giants pitcher Ramon Ramirez was called an "illegal alien" by a sports talk-radio host.[2] He was not in the US illegally; he was in the country via a relatively common employment visa. In another case, ESPN fired radio host Colin Cowherd when he remarked that baseball is not a "thinking-man's game" because so many of the players come from the Dominican Republic.[3]

As anti-immigrant rhetoric spread in the 2010s, some professional athletes took a stand. A new

RACISM IN SOCCER

Soccer, the most popular international sport, has a long history of encountering racism. In 2009, Inter Milan fans supported striker Mario Balotelli when he was faced with racist abuse by opposing fans. In 2013, AC Milan's Kevin-Prince Boateng led his team off the field because of racist chants in the crowd. "Shame that these things still happen," he tweeted.[4]

generation of athletes was ready to use its platform to speak about social justice.

BOYCOTT!

In 2010, Arizona passed the Support Our Law Enforcement and Safe Neighborhoods Act (SB 1070). SB 1070 gave law enforcement officers the right to stop anyone and demand proof that the person was in the country legally. People across the country were enraged at legislation that they believed encouraged racial profiling and harassment.

The Arizona Diamondbacks faced much of this anger as they played baseball in stadiums across the country. Owner Ken Kendrick was a supporter of the Republican legislators behind the new law. He denied he supported SB 1070. But he held fundraisers for the Republican Party at the Diamondbacks stadium. Crowds gathered at Diamondback games in other states. They demanded that the 2011 MLB All-Star Game be moved out of Arizona.

Latino baseball players also took a stand. José Guillén of the Kansas City Royals said, "I've never seen anything like that in the United States. . . . I hope police aren't going to stop every dark-skinned person."[5] The MLB players' union pointed out that there were international players on the Diamondbacks team. The union said that it would "consider additional steps . . . to protect the rights and interests of our members."[6]

Phoenix guard Steve Nash wears one of the team's early "Los Suns" jerseys, an effort to reach out to Arizona's Latino community.

The Phoenix Suns basketball organization stood behind the protesters. On Cinco de Mayo, a major Mexican holiday, Suns players wore jerseys that said "Los Suns" to protest the legislation. Guard Steve Nash, who had spoken out against the war in Iraq in 2003, became the players' spokesman on the issue.

The Suns' involvement marked a new wave of activism in sports. The NBA players' union supported the players. The Suns' activism sparked a protest outside the stadium with even the Phoenix mayor wearing a "Los Suns" jersey. Fans watching the game on television across the country saw the protest.

In Georgia, which had just passed a similar bill, MLB held its Civil Rights Game. The league had decided to honor rock guitarist Carlos Santana. When he took the microphone, Santana declared that the people of both Arizona and Georgia should be ashamed of themselves. The crowd booed.

The call for a boycott of Arizona for the MLB All-Star Game continued. The league stood its ground, refusing to give in to the protests. Those who demanded the game be moved finally gave up. The courts had struck down parts of SB 1070, and the players and public who had rallied against racial profiling had to be content with that.

BLACK LIVES MATTER

In 2012, the statistics on young black men facing profiling, incarceration, and unemployment were abysmal. People of color made up 30 percent of the population that year, but 60 percent of the prison population. The Department of

BLACK LIVES MATTER TIMELINE

- George Zimmerman shoots Trayvon Martin (age 17) in Sanford, Florida, on February 26, 2012.

- Eric Garner (age 27) is killed by police in Staten Island, New York, on July 17, 2014.

- Michael Brown (age 18) is shot by police in Ferguson, Missouri, on August 9, 2014.

- Tamir Rice (age 12) is shot by police on a playground in Cleveland, Ohio, on November 22, 2014.

- Walter Scott (age 50) is shot by police in North Charleston, South Carolina, on April 4, 2015.

- Freddie Gray Jr. (age 25) dies in police custody in Baltimore, Maryland, in April 2015.

- Sandra Bland (age 28) dies in police custody in Waller County, Texas, on July 13, 2015.

- Alton Sterling (age 37) is shot by police in Baton Rouge, Louisiana, on July 5, 2016.

- Philando Castile (age 32) is shot by police during a traffic stop in Falcon Heights, Minnesota, on July 6, 2016.

- Five police officers are killed by a sniper at a Black Lives Matter protest in Dallas, Texas, on July 7, 2016.

Justice found that Hispanics were three times more likely to be searched during a traffic stop than white people. Black people were twice as likely to be arrested and four times as likely to have force used against them by police. Human Rights Watch found that black people accounted for 14 percent of regular drug users but 37 percent of those arrested for drug offenses.

Black professional athletes were aware of these problems. Many of them had their own stories to tell about encounters with the police. A Houston police officer pulled a gun on NFL player Ryan Moats and his wife in a hospital parking lot when they were visiting his wife's mother. Robbie Tolan, a minor league baseball player, was confronted by police with guns when he and a cousin pulled into his driveway in their affluent neighborhood. Tolan's mother came out of the house to explain that the car and home were theirs. When police pushed his mother, Tolan went to her defense and was shot in the chest.

Yet it took the case of Trayvon Martin to motivate highly paid athletes to return to protest racial discrimination against the black community. As people in cities across America crowded the streets to protest the killing of the Florida teenager in 2012, black players returned to using their platform to protest racial injustice. When Kaepernick took a knee during the playing of the national anthem, he was not alone. He was not even the first.

THE BEGINNING

Months earlier, in March, LeBron James and eight other members of the Miami Heat basketball team posed for a picture wearing hoodies. They sent it out on Twitter in remembrance of what Martin was wearing the night he was killed. Heat guard Dwyane Wade wrote "We Want Justice" on his shoe for their game on March 23. The NBA players' association came out in support of the players. Others, such as NFL star Jamaal Charles, used social media to air protests.

A message scrawled on the shoe of Miami Heat guard Dwyane Wade refers to the Trayvon Martin shooting in 2012.

Over the next years, more incidents of police brutality made the news. Black athletes took a stand. In 2014, NBA teams wore "I Can't Breathe" shirts during warm-ups. The phrase was a protest against the police brutality that had killed Eric Garner in New York. They were his last words before he suffocated.

In 2015, racial unrest at the University of Missouri resulted in the resignation of university president Tim Wolfe. Students had protested for months as instances of racism were ignored. Finally graduate student Jonathan Butler decided to go on a hunger strike to bring attention to the problem of racism on campus. Members of the football team got behind Butler, saying they would not play until Wolfe stepped down. Canceling the football season would have cost the university millions of dollars. Wolfe stepped down two days later.[7]

Black female athletes, whose platform for protest had grown since the 1960s, also spoke out. Women of the Women's National Basketball Association (WNBA) wore #BlackLivesMatter T-shirts during their pregame warm-ups in 2016. Players from the league champion Minnesota Lynx wore shirts reading "Change starts with us—Justice & Accountability" to protest the police shootings of Philando Castile and Alton Sterling in July 2016. Their shirts also honored the five Dallas, Texas, police officers who were murdered in the aftermath of those two shootings.

IMMIGRANT ATHLETES

Colleges and professional teams have begun recruiting international athletes to play in the United States. There are more than 17,000 international student athletes in NCAA schools.[8] For professional teams, it is often cheaper to identify and train athletes overseas before bringing them to America to play ball. In 2017, 29.8 percent of MLB players did not come from the US mainland. Sixteen players came from US territory Puerto Rico, but the largest numbers came from the Dominican Republic, Venezuela, and Cuba.[9]

THE NEW OLYMPIANS

Rio de Janeiro, Brazil, hosted the Olympic Games in

Minnesota Lynx players Rebekkah Brunson, left, and Natasha Howard wear T-shirts in support of Black Lives Matter and the slain Dallas police officers.

August 2016. Before the events began, people protesting police brutality in Brazil marched in the streets. Some US activists in the Black Lives Matter protests joined them.

But a Reuters/Ipsos poll taken just before the Games showed that most Americans didn't want protests at the Olympic Games. Sixty-five percent of Americans thought that athletes should not express political opinions at the Games. The figure was fifty-two percent among racial minorities.[10]

The 2016 Olympics still included athletes who used their public positions to address racism. Ibtihaj Muhammad, a fencer, was the first US woman to compete in the Olympics in a hijab. She spoke up about Donald Trump's anti-immigration comments. She also addressed her

Ibtihaj Muhammad was the first US Olympic athlete to compete in a hijab when she won a bronze medal in fencing at the 2016 Rio Games.

concerns over racial injustice she had experienced. "It's ridiculous and we as a country have to change, and I feel like this is our moment," she said.[11]

Simone Manuel also made history in Rio. She became the first black woman from the United States to win an individual gold medal in swimming. She spoke up about police brutality. "It means a lot, especially with what is going on in the world today, some of the issues of police brutality. This win hopefully brings hope and change to some of the issues that are going on. My color just comes with the territory."[12]

But it was Kaepernick's actions that fall that became the movement's iconic emblem. His kneeling during the national anthem once again brought the question of sports, politics, and protest to the attention of the nation.

DISCUSSION STARTERS

- Do you think the current wave of immigrant sports players will change racist attitudes?
- What effect do you think stereotyping has on who participates in which sports and what positions they play?
- How do you think economics determines how players are chosen for teams?

CHAPTER EIGHT

HEROES OR VILLAINS?

P olitical commentary by people with public platforms such as actors, musicians, bloggers, and athletes is not new. Those who have strong opinions about issues often feel it is their duty to use the platform they have. Celebrities fight for causes that are important to them, and they use their platforms to raise money for causes such as fighting cancer or saving the environment. Others, often those who disagree with them, believe performers should stick to what they do best and leave politics to politicians.

People who stand up for a cause take a risk. Public backlash can cost them millions of dollars and even end their careers. The spring after Kaepernick's protest, he became a free agent and left the 49ers. Although he was coming off a strong season, no NFL team offered him a contract for the next season.

Many claimed he was not a good fit for their program. Others claimed he was past his peak in football. But many felt that he was being blackballed for his political protest. In October 2017, Kaepernick filed a grievance with the NFL for colluding to keep him out of the league.

Having come full circle, Muhammad Ali prepares to light the Olympic flame before the 1996 Atlanta Games.

LESSONS OF HISTORY

The passage of time has made some sports protesters into icons of civil rights. In 1971, the US Supreme Court overturned Muhammad Ali's conviction for dodging the draft. He regained his heavyweight champion title. After his retirement, he stayed involved in civil rights and became one of the most beloved figures in the world. In 1996, he lit the torch at the Olympic Games in Atlanta, Georgia. In 1999, he was featured on the cover of the Wheaties box, the cultural equivalent of a gold medal for athletes. In 2005, he received the Presidential Medal of Freedom.

Sports Illustrated reported that the photograph of Tommie Smith and John Carlos with fists raised on the podium in 1968 is the most reproduced image in the history of the Olympics. Both men went on to play professional football. Smith earned a degree in social science from San Jose State in 1969 and a master's in sociology from the Goddard-Cambridge Graduate Program in Social Change in Boston in 1976. He interviewed for a track coaching job at Santa Monica College in 1978. He didn't think he had a chance at the job but got it and spent 27 years coaching.[1]

Carlos became a counselor at Palm Springs High School. Now retired, he continues to give speeches encouraging support for

BROWNS TAKE A KNEE

In August 2017 a white supremacist drove a car into a group of protesters in Charlottesville, Virginia. One person was killed and several were injured. In response, some of the Cleveland Browns knelt in a prayer circle during the playing of the national anthem. Tight end Seth DeValve, a white man married to a black woman, knelt with his teammates. He explained, "I myself will be raising children that don't look like me, and I want to do my part as well to do everything I can to raise them in a better environment than we have right now. So I wanted to take the opportunity with my teammates during the anthem to pray for our country and also to draw attention to the fact that we have work to do."[2]

civil rights. Smith and Carlos were honored by President Barack Obama along with the 2016 Olympic team at the White House.

Lee Evans had won gold in the 1968 Olympic Games in the 400-meter race and the 4x400-meter relay. But he lost his chance to compete in 1972 when Vince Matthews and Wayne Collett were expelled from the Games for disrespecting the flag. Evans went on to coach track teams in Africa. Upon his return to the United States he became director of athletics for Special Olympics International.

DOES IT MAKE A DIFFERENCE?

Colin Kaepernick had many supporters after his protest in 2016. Each week more players

SOCCER PROTEST

Soccer star Megan Rapinoe of the US Women's National Team was the first white athlete to kneel in solidarity with Kaepernick. As a gay woman, she knows what it means to not be treated equally in society. She also believes that other white athletes should do more to stand up for injustice in the black community. Rapinoe took a knee while the anthem played before a National Women's Soccer League game between her Seattle Reign and the Chicago Red Stars. The next week, the teams were kept in the locker room during the playing of the anthem. After Rapinoe repeated the gesture at an international game, the US Soccer Federation passed a rule that required all players to stand at national matches. Rapinoe agreed to abide by the rule, but wrote, "When I take a knee, I am facing the flag with my full body, staring straight into the heart of our country's ultimate symbol of freedom—because I believe it is my responsibility, just as it is yours, to ensure that freedom is afforded to everyone in this country."[3]

US soccer star Megan Rapinoe takes a knee during the national anthem before a game in September 2016.

knelt, linked arms, or put their hands on the shoulders of those kneeling in support.

In October, the NFL owners met with a group of 40 players to discuss police brutality and justice reform. Kaepernick was not invited. But the owners offered to donate nearly $100 million to "causes considered important to African American communities."[4]

Kaepernick was runner-up for *Time* magazine's Person of the Year in 2016. He was named *GQ* magazine's Citizen of the Year. He won the 2017 *Sports Illustrated* Muhammad Ali Legacy Award. But no team wanted to sign him.

There were only a few protesters at the start of the 2017 season. That changed after President Trump attacked the protesters at a rally. He called them a vulgar name and said they should be fired. The next week, more than 100 players knelt during the anthem. The Dallas Cowboys and the team's owner, Jerry Jones, knelt together even though Jones had earlier threatened to discipline players who kneeled. On the other side of the argument, some fans burned season tickets and refused to watch NFL games.[5]

Fans, management, and athletes disagreed on whether politics, protest, and sports went together. But there was no doubt that sports had a powerful impact on society—and athletes could use their voices if they chose.

DISCUSSION STARTERS

- Other public gatherings such as movies, concerts, and plays—even Fourth of July fireworks shows—do not begin with the playing of the national anthem. Do you think the anthem should be played at all public events? Why or why not?

- How do you think President Trump's involvement in the NFL protests was like or unlike Avery Brundage's involvement in Olympic protests?

- How do you think Colin Kaepernick will be viewed by most people in 20 years? Will he be remembered more for football or social justice?

SIGNIFICANT EVENTS

○ At the 1936 Berlin Olympics, German dictator Adolf Hitler attempts to demonstrate his racist beliefs by showcasing white athletes' talent. African American athlete Jesse Owens proves him wrong with his stellar medal-winning performance at the Games.

○ Major League Baseball refuses to sign black players, leaving them to fend for themselves in the Negro Leagues. In 1947, Jackie Robinson breaks the color barrier when he debuts for the Brooklyn Dodgers. He becomes one of the team's best players, winning the National League Rookie of the Year Award.

○ Boxer Cassius Clay wins a gold medal at the 1960 Summer Olympics. He goes on to win the world heavyweight championship, changes his name to Muhammad Ali, and becomes one of the most important figures in sports history for his excellence in the ring and his advocacy for civil rights for all people outside the ring.

○ The 1968 Summer Olympics in Mexico City are held amid growing racial tension around the world, especially in the United States. US sprinters Tommie Smith and John Carlos raise their black-gloved fists on the medal stand while the national anthem is played. Their protest adds fuel to the national conversation about race.

○ A series of high-profile police shootings of unarmed black men spark unrest throughout the United States in the summer of 2016. San Francisco 49ers quarterback Colin Kaepernick becomes a symbol of the protest by kneeling during the playing of the national anthem. He is joined by some teammates and opponents, and the protest spills over into the political arena in 2017 as President Donald Trump criticizes the players.

KEY PLAYERS

○ Jesse Owens becomes a national hero, winning four gold medals at the 1936 Berlin Olympics.

○ Jackie Robinson breaks the color barrier in baseball in 1947.

○ Muhammad Ali is convicted of dodging the draft in 1967, receives a five-year prison sentence, and is stripped of his world title.

○ Tommie Smith and John Carlos are expelled from the 1968 Olympic Games in Mexico City for protesting racism.

○ Colin Kaepernick takes a knee during the national anthem to protest police brutality in 2016.

IMPACT ON SOCIETY

The sports world has many of the same problems found in the rest of society. Black and other minority athletes have suffered the same racism within their fields as minorities in the greater society. Athletes have used their high-profile platforms to speak out about civil rights and racial injustice.

QUOTE

"I have to stand up for people that are oppressed. . . . If they take football away, my endorsements from me, I know that I stood up for what is right."

—*Colin Kaepernick*

GLOSSARY

acquitted
Found not guilty of a criminal act.

amateur
A person who competes in a sport without payment.

apartheid
The historic policy of segregation in South Africa.

Aryan race
A racial group including people of northern European descent that Adolf Hitler and the Nazis believed to be a master race.

assassination
The killing of a prominent person for political or religious reasons.

backlash
A strong and adverse reaction to a social or political event by a large number of people.

blackballed
Rejected, usually in a secretive way.

boycott
A refusal to have dealings with another group, usually in order to express disapproval or to force acceptance of certain conditions.

colluding
Secretly working together with the intent of cheating someone or something.

commodity
Something that has value and is bought and sold.

discrimination
Unfair treatment of other people, usually because of race, age, or gender.

draft
A system in which people of a certain age are required to register for military service.

induction

The process of placing someone into the armed services.

integrate

To make schools, parks, and other facilities available to people of all races on an equal basis.

intolerance

An inability to accept views that are at odds with one's own.

norm

A social behavior that is typical or expected.

ostracized

Shunned or otherwise excluded from a society or a group.

podium

A small platform where people stand to be recognized.

revenue

Income, especially of a company or organization and of a substantial nature.

segregated

Separated based on race, gender, ethnicity, or other factors.

sociology

The study of human society.

taunt

A remark made to anger, wound, or provoke someone.

vilify

To speak or write about someone in an abusive manner.

ADDITIONAL RESOURCES

SELECTED BIBLIOGRAPHY

Blake, James. *Ways of Grace: Stories of Activism, Adversity, and How Sports Can Bring Us Together*. HarperCollins, 2017.

Hartmann, Douglas. *Race, Culture, and the Revolt of the Black Athlete: The 1968 Olympic Protests and Their Aftermath*. University of Chicago, 2003.

Zirin, Dave. *Game Over: How Politics Has Turned the Sports World Upside Down*. New Press, 2013.

FURTHER READINGS

Ali, Hana. *Ali on Ali: Why He Said What He Said When He Said It*. Workman, 2018.

Biles, Simone. *Courage to Soar: A Body in Motion, a Life in Balance*. Zondervan, 2016.

Sheinkin, Steve. *Undefeated: Jim Thorpe and the Carlisle Indian School Football Team*. Roaring Brook, 2017.

Thomas, Etan. *We Matter: Athletes and Activism*. Edge of Sports, 2018.

ONLINE RESOURCES

Booklinks
NONFICTION NETWORK
FREE! ONLINE NONFICTION RESOURCES

To learn more about politics and protest in sports, visit abdobooklinks.com. These links are routinely monitored and updated to provide the most current information available.

MORE INFORMATION

For more information on this subject, contact or visit the following organizations:

JACKIE ROBINSON MUSEUM
1 Hudson Square
75 Varick Street, Second Floor
New York, NY 10013-1917
212-290-8600
jackierobinson.org/about/museum

This museum was founded as a memorial to Jackie Robinson and his achievements.

NATIONAL MUSEUM OF AFRICAN AMERICAN HISTORY AND CULTURE
1400 Constitution Avenue NW
Washington, DC 20560
844-750-3012
nmaahc.si.edu

One of the top museums in Washington, the National Museum of African American History and Culture is dedicated to black contributions to history and culture in the United States.

SOURCE NOTES

CHAPTER 1. WHO IS MORE PATRIOTIC?

1. Euan McKirdy. "NFL Star Colin Kaepernick Sits in Protest during National Anthem." *CNN*, 28 Aug. 2016. CNN.com. Accessed 23 July 2018.

2. Chelsea J. Carter and Holly Yan. "Why This Verdict? Five Things That Led to Zimmerman's Acquittal." *CNN*, 5 July 2013. CNN.com. Accessed 23 July 2018.

3. Stephen Moore. "Why Sports and Politics Do Not Mix." *Washington Times*, 8 Oct. 2017. washingtontimes.com. Accessed 23 July 2018.

4. Mike Snider. "Are NFL Player Protests 'Massively, Massively' Hurting TV Ratings?" *USA Today*, 26 Sept. 2017. usatoday.com. Accessed 23 July 2018.

5. "National Football League (NFL)—Statistics and Facts. *Statista*, 2018. statista.com. Accessed 23 July 2018.

6. Charlotte Wilder. "Donald Trump Says Colin Kaepernick Should Find a New Country." *USA Today*, 30 Aug. 2016. usatoday.com. Accessed 23 July 2018.

7. Terry Gross. "'I Can't Breathe' Examines Modern Policing and the Life and Death of Eric Garner." *National Public Radio*, 23 Oct. 2017. npr.org. Accessed 23 July 2018.

8. McKirdy, "NFL Star Colin Kaepernick Sits in Protest During National Anthem."

CHAPTER 2. THE BEGINNING OF INTEGRATION

1. Sarah Kaplan. "Jack Johnson, World's First Black Boxing Champion, Was Jailed under Jim Crow. Will He Get a Posthumous Pardon?" *Washington Post*, 5 Feb. 2016. washingtonpost.com. Accessed 23 July 2018.

2. Sally Jenkins. "Why Are Jim Thorpe's Olympic Records Still Not Recognized?" *Smithsonian Magazine*, July 2012. smithsonianmag.com. Accessed 23 July 2018.

3. Biography.com editors. "Jesse Owens Biography." *Biography.com*, 2 Apr. 2014. biography.com. Accessed 23 July 2018.

4. "Chicago Bombs." *Smithsonian National Postal Museum*, n.d. postalmuseum.si.edu. Accessed 23 July 2018.

5. Jose Martinez. "25 Black Athletes Who Changed the World." *Complex*, 9 Feb. 2012. complex.com. Accessed 23 July 2018.

6. "Jackie Robinson." *National Baseball Hall of Fame*, n.d. baseballhall.org. Accessed 23 July 2018.

7. Harry Gordon. "Arthur Ashe Has to Be Aware That He Is a Pioneer in Short White Pants." *New York Times*, 22 Aug. 2013. nytimes.com. Accessed 23 July 2018.

CHAPTER 3. THE RISE OF PROTEST

1. Doug Merlino. "Bill Russell, Civil Rights Hero and Inventor of Airborne Basketball." *Bleacher Report*, 29 Apr. 2011. bleacherreport.com. Accessed 23 July 2018.

2. Arica L. Coleman. "What's in a Name: Meet the Original Cassius Clay." *Time*, 10 June 2016. time.com. Accessed 23 July 2018.

3. Krishnadev Calamur. "Muhammad Ali and Vietnam." *Atlantic*, 4 June 2016. theatlantic.com. Accessed 23 July 2018.

4. Tom Valentine. "Vietnam War Draft." *Vietnam War*, 25 July 2013. thevietnamwar.info. Accessed 23 July 2018.

5. Valentine, "Vietnam War Draft."

6. Valentine, "Vietnam War Draft."

7. "Vietnam War Casualties by Race, Ethnicity, and Natl Origin." *American War Library*, n.d. americanwarlibrary.com. Accessed 23 July 2018.

8. Calamur, "Muhammad Ali and Vietnam."

9. Gerald F. Goodwin. "Black and White in Vietnam." *New York Times*, 18 July 2017. nytimes.com. Accessed 23 July 2018.

10. Biography.com editors. "Althea Gibson Biography." *Biography.com*, 2 Apr. 2014. biography.com. Accessed 23 July 2018.

11. Biography.com editors. "Wilma Rudolph Biography." *Biography.com*, 2 Apr. 2014. biography.com. Accessed 23 July 2018.

12. Ashley Farmer. "Black Women Athletes, Protest, and Politics: An Interview with Amira Rose Davis." *Black Perspectives*, 14 Oct. 2016. aaihs.org. Accessed 23 July 2018.

CHAPTER 4. ATHLETES TAKE A STAND

1. Dave Zirin. "The Explosive 1968 Olympics." *International Socialist Review*, Issue 61, Sept.–Oct. 2008. isreview.org. Accessed 23 July 2018.

2. Christopher S. Wren. "South Africa a Bit Closer to Rejoining Olympics." *New York Times*, 28 Mar. 1991. nytimes.com. Accessed 23 July 2018.

3. Douglas Hartmann. *Race, Culture, and the Revolt of the Black Athlete: The 1968 Olympic Protests and Their Aftermath.* University of Chicago, 2003. 34.

4. Ryan Vooris. "10 Athletes Who Made Bold Political and Social Statements." *Bleacher Report*, 30 Aug 2010. bleacherreport.com. Accessed 23 July 2018.

CHAPTER 5. THE WORLD STAGE

1. Dave Zirin. "The Explosive 1968 Olympics." *International Socialist Review*, Issue 61, Sept.–Oct. 2008. isreview.org. Accessed 23 July 2018.

2. Zirin, "The Explosive 1968 Olympics."

3. Louis Jacobson. "A Short History of the National Anthem, Protests and the NFL." Politifact, 25 Sept. 2017. politifact.com. Accessed 23 July 2018.

4. James Blake. *Ways of Grace: Stories of Activism, Adversity, and How Sports Can Bring Us Together.* HarperCollins, 2017. 43.

5. Claire Noland. "Wayne Collett Dies at 60; UCLA Sprinter Won Silver Medal at '72 Olympics." *Los Angeles Times*, 17 Mar. 2010. latimes.com. Accessed 23 July 2018.

CHAPTER 6. THE BUSINESS OF SPORT

1. David Steele. "Ex-NFL Anthem Protestor Applauds Colin Kaepernick and Athletes Supporting Him." *Sporting News*, 6 Sept. 2016. sportingnews.com. Accessed 23 July 2018.

2. Douglas Hartmann. *Race, Culture, and the Revolt of the Black Athlete: The 1968 Olympic Protests and Their Aftermath.* University of Chicago, 2003. 178.

3. "Star-Spangled Coercion." Editorial. *New York Times*, 15 Mar. 1996. nytimes.com. Accessed 23 July 2018.

4. Ryan Vooris. "10 Athletes Who Made Bold Political and Social Statements." *Bleacher Report*, 30 Aug 2010. bleacherreport.com. Accessed 23 July 2018.

5. Dave Zirin. *Game Over: How Politics Has Turned the Sports World Upside Down.* New Press, 2013. 110.

6. Zirin, *Game Over*, 111.

7. Zirin, *Game Over*, 111.

8. Jake New. "Graduation Gap for Black Football Players." *Inside Higher Ed*, 19 Oct. 2016. insidehighered.com. Accessed 23 July 2018

9. "NCAA Finances." *USA Today*, n.d. usatoday.com. Accessed 22 July 2018.

10. Zirin, *Game Over*, 113.

11. Mona Chalabi. "Three Leagues, 92 Teams, and One Black Principal Owner." *FiveThirtyEight*, 28 Apr. 2014. fivethirtyeight.com. Accessed 23 July 2018.

12. John Keim. "With Average NFL Career 3.3 Years, Players Motivated to Complete MBA Program." *ESPN*, 29 July 2016. espn.com. Accessed 23 July 2018.

13. Christian Davenport. "The Pentagon Paid Lucrative Sports Franchises Millions to Honor Troops." *Washington Post*, 4 Nov. 2015. washingtonpost.com. Accessed 23 July 2018.

14. Eyder Peralta. "Pentagon Paid Sports Teams Millions for 'Paid Patriotism' Events." *National Public Radio*, 5 Nov. 2015. npr.org. Accessed 23 July 2018.

15. Sen. John McCain and Sen. Jeff Flake. "Tackling Paid Patriotism: A Joint Oversight Report." *John McCain US Senate Website*. 4 Nov. 2015. mccain.senate.gov. Accessed 23 July 2018.

16. Peralta, "Pentagon Paid Sports Teams Millions for 'Paid Patriotism' Events."

CHAPTER 7. RACISM CONTINUES

1. Mona Chalabi. "Three Leagues, 92 Teams, and One Black Principal Owner." *FiveThirtyEight*, 28 Apr. 2014. fivethirtyeight.com. Accessed 23 July 2018.

2. Henry Schulman. "SF Giants' Bochy: Tony Bruno's Comment Racist." *San Francisco Chronicle*, 7 Aug. 2011. sfgate.com. Accessed 23 July 2018.

3. Bryan Llenas. "ESPN Yanks Colin Cowherd off the Air after He Insults Dominicans." *Fox News*, 24 July 2015. foxnews.com. Accessed 23 July 2018.

4. "A Timeline of Social Activism in Sports." *CNN*, 9 Jan. 2018. cnn.com. Accessed 23 July 2018.

5. Dave Zirin. *Game Over: How Politics Has Turned the Sports World Upside Down*. New Press, 2013. 124.

6. Zirin, *Game Over*, 124–125.

7. Rohan Nadkarni and Alex Nieves. "Why Missouri's Football Team Joined a Protest against School Administration." *Sports Illustrated*, 9 Nov. 2015. si.com. Accessed 23 July 2018.

8. "International Student-Athletes." *National Collegiate Athletic Association*, n.d. ncaa.org. Accessed 23 July 2018.

9. Bill Baer. "29.8% of Players on 2017 Opening Day Rosters Born outside the U.S., Setting New Record." *NBC Sports*, 3 Apr. 2017. mlb.nbcsports.com. Accessed 23 July 2018.

10. Ben Rosen. "Do Black Lives Matter Protests Belong at the Olympic Games?" *Christian Science Monitor*, 1 Aug. 2016. csmonitor.com. Accessed 23 July 2018.

11. Olivia Blair. "Rio 2016: US Muslim Fencer 'Doesn't Feel Safe' Due to Anti-Muslim Sentiment in America." *Independent*, 5 Aug. 2016. independent.co.uk. Accessed 23 July 2018.

12. Martin Rogers. "American Simone Manuel Speaks Out on Police Brutality, Race after Earning Olympic Gold." *USA Today*,12 Aug. 2016. usatoday.com. Accessed 23 July 2018.

CHAPTER 8. HEROES OR VILLAINS?

1. David Davis. "Olympic Athletes Who Took a Stand." *Smithsonian Magazine*, Aug. 2008. smithsonianmag.com. Accessed 23 July 2018.

2. Pat McManamon. "12 Browns Players Kneel in Prayer over Racial, Social Injustice." *ESPN*, 22 Aug. 2017. espn.com. Accessed 23 July 2018.

3. Andrew Joseph. "Megan Rapinoe Won't Fight U.S. Soccer's New Anthem Policy after Taking a Knee in 2016." *USA Today*, 6 Mar. 2017. usatoday.com. Accessed 23 July 2018.

4. Priscilla Totiyapungprasert. "Is Colin Kaepernick at Super Bowl 2018? His Future in the NFL Is Uncertain." *Bustle*, 4 Feb 2018. bustle.com. Accessed 23 July 2018.

5. John Branch. "National Anthem Protests Sidelined by Ambiguity." *New York Times*, 1 Jan. 2018. nytimes.com. Accessed 23 July 2018.

INDEX

DUCHESS HARRIS, JD, PHD

Professor Harris is the chair of the American Studies department at Macalester College and curator of the Duchess Harris Collection of ABDO books. She is the author and coauthor of recently released ABDO books including *Hidden Human Computers: The Black Women of NASA*, *Black Lives Matter*, and *Race and Policing*.

Before working with ABDO, she authored several other books on the topics of race, culture, and American history. She served as an associate editor for *Litigation News*, the American Bar Association Section of Litigation's quarterly flagship publication, and was the first editor in chief of *Law Raza*, an interactive online journal covering race and the law, published at William Mitchell College of Law. She has earned a PhD in American Studies from the University of Minnesota and a JD from William Mitchell College of Law.

CYNTHIA KENNEDY HENZEL

Cynthia Kennedy Henzel has a BS in social studies education and an MS in geography. She has worked as a teacher-educator in many countries. Currently, she writes fiction and nonfiction and also develops educational materials for social studies, history, science, and ELL students. She has written more than 85 books for young people.